WONDERFUL
WORLD OF
ANIMALS

This 1997 edition published by Brockhampton Press
20 Bloomsbury Street, London WC1B 3QA

Text by Beatrice MacLeod
Designed by Marco Nardi
Illustrated by Paola Holguín

Created and produced by McRae Books Srl
Via dei Rustici, 5 – Florence, Italy

ISBN 1-86019-586-5

WONDERFUL WORLD OF ANIMALS

INSECTS
and other INVERTEBRATES

Beatrice MacLeod
Illustrated by Paola Holguín

BROCKHAMPTON PRESS

INVERTEBRATES

Invertebrates constitute over ninety percent of all animal species. They differ from vertebrates (mammals, fish, birds, reptiles and amphibians) because they lack a backbone. This is the only thing that all members of the huge and varied group of invertebrates have in common.

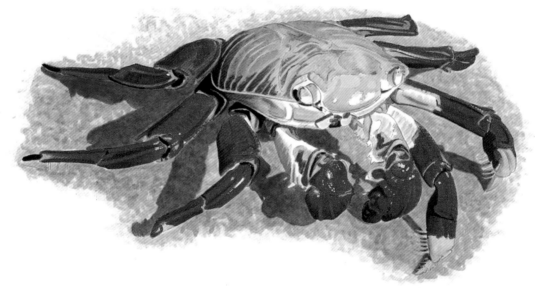

Crustaceans, including crabs, shrimps and lobsters, are the most successful marine invertebrates. Crabs have 5 pairs of claws. The large front pincers are used mainly for feeding, while the others are used for walking.

Galapagos red crab

Snails, slugs, oysters, clams, octopuses and squid are all invertebrates of the **mollusc** group. Most molluscs have hard shells to protect them. A snail's shell is spiral-shaped and is all in one piece. The shells of some other molluscs, like oysters or clams, are divided in two pieces.

Snail

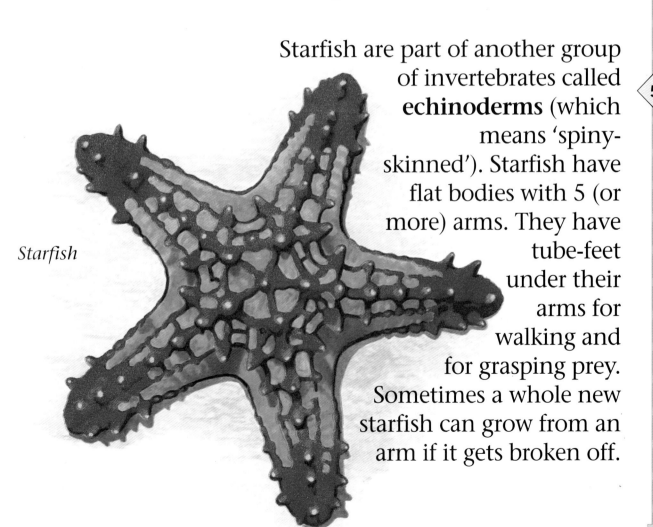

Starfish

Starfish are part of another group of invertebrates called **echinoderms** (which means 'spiny-skinned'). Starfish have flat bodies with 5 (or more) arms. They have tube-feet under their arms for walking and for grasping prey. Sometimes a whole new starfish can grow from an arm if it gets broken off.

WHAT IS AN INSECT?

Insects are the largest group of invertebrates. They vary greatly in size and appearance, but they all have some things in common, such as the hard cuticle covering on their bodies and legs. This is called an exoskeleton (outside skeleton). An insect's body is divided in three parts: head, thorax and abdomen.

Silverfish

Nymphalid butterfly

Butterflies are winged insects with distinctive club-tipped antennae. Unlike moths, butterflies are usually brightly coloured and are active during the day.

Ants occur worldwide, although most live in hot climates. Like all insects, they have six legs; each pair is connected to one of the three parts of the body.

Red ant

The **silverfish** is a flat wingless insect. Its body is covered with silvery scales. It lives indoors and likes to eat paper (including books and wallpaper) and fabrics.

Stag beetle

Stag beetles have a robust shell and are usually black or brown. They have antennae on their heads. Male beetles have two huge mandibles (jaws) which resemble the antlers of a stag.

PLANT OR ANIMAL?

Plants feed themselves by making energy from sunlight. Animals feed on plants or other animals. Most animals move to catch their food. Some invertebrates, such as sponges or coral, are attached to the sea floor and wait for food to arrive on sea currents.

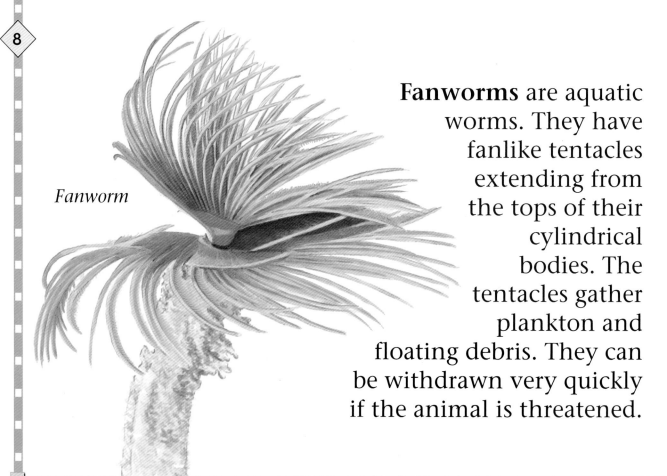

Fanworm

Fanworms are aquatic worms. They have fanlike tentacles extending from the tops of their cylindrical bodies. The tentacles gather plankton and floating debris. They can be withdrawn very quickly if the animal is threatened.

Sponges are primitive aquatic animals. There are about 5,000 different species. They nearly all live in the sea. They live in colonies or alone, attached to the sea floor or other hard surfaces. They feed on tiny organisms and debris which they absorb through the skin.

Tube sponge

9

Corals are simple organisms made up of large numbers of tiny animals called polyps. They grow in shallow tropical seas. Polyps feed on plankton, trapping it in their tentacles. As the polyps die new ones grow on top. Gradually they form large reefs.

Coral

SUCCESSFUL ANIMALS

Invertebrates have been very successful. They have adapted to even the most difficult conditions and have populated every corner of the Earth. The smaller species live on land or in the air. Some marine species are huge; the giant squid grows up to 18 metres long!

Sea urchin

Sea urchins live on the sea floor. They use their tube feet and long spines to move about. Their mouths, on the underside of their bodies, have tough teeth which they use to scrape algae and other food from rocks.

Spiders are different from insects because they don't have antennae or wings, and because they have eight legs (rather than six). Spiders all have silk glands and emit droplets of silk to form threads. A spider's body is divided in two parts – the *prosoma* and the *abdomen* – connected by a narrow stalk.

Striped argiope spider

Reproduction

Invertebrates reproduce in a number of different ways. Many insects, corals, jellyfish, molluscs and crustaceans lay eggs. Others, including sponges, duplicate a part of themselves which then grows into a new individual.

INSECTS EVERYWHERE

There are more different species of insects than there are of all the other animals put together. Scientists have not discovered and named all the species yet. Insects live almost everywhere, from tropical jungles to the polar regions. Some insects even live in the sea.

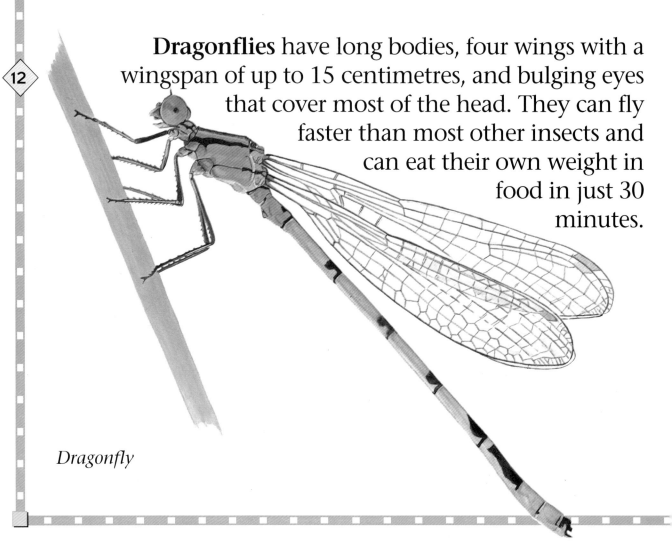

Dragonflies have long bodies, four wings with a wingspan of up to 15 centimetres, and bulging eyes that cover most of the head. They can fly faster than most other insects and can eat their own weight in food in just 30 minutes.

Dragonfly

The **diving beetle** stores a supply of air under its wings which it uses to breathe underwater. When this supply is finished, it raises its abdomen out of the water and breathes through its spiracles. Diving beetles prey on insects and other aquatic animals, including fish larger than themselves.

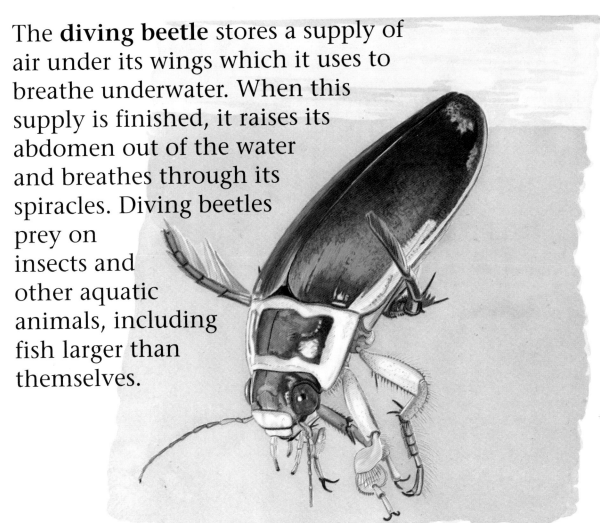

Diving beetle

Insects' eyes

Insects have large compound eyes made up of thousands of tiny lenses, all packed in closely together. As well as compound eyes, many insects also have simple eyes, called *ocelli*, which are sensitive to changes in light.

INVERTEBRATE HOMES

Many invertebrates, like snails and clams, have protective shells on their backs. They go inside when danger threatens. Others, such as wasps, bees, termites and ants, build complicated nests which require great home-building skills.

Nautilus

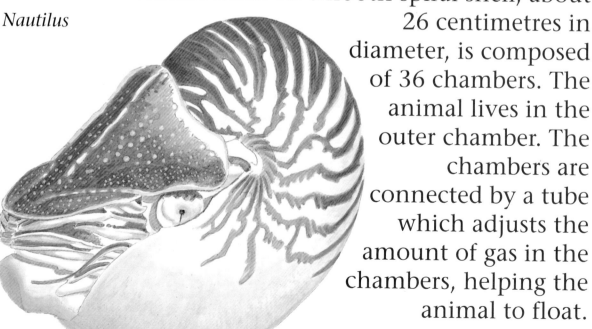

The **nautilus** is a small mollusc with an external shell. Its smooth spiral shell, about 26 centimetres in diameter, is composed of 36 chambers. The animal lives in the outer chamber. The chambers are connected by a tube which adjusts the amount of gas in the chambers, helping the animal to float.

Tiny **termites** build mounds many thousands of times larger than themselves. Termites need a constant temperature to survive and their mounds are perfectly designed to regulate heat and humidity. A complex system of chambers and corridors creates a well-ventilated environment. Inside, the queen termite lays eggs, while worker termites bring food and look after the mound and soldier termites guard it.

Soldier termite guarding a termite mound

FEEDING

Ladybird

Some insects are herbivores and others are carnivores. Both types play a special role in plant and human life. Nectar feeders carry pollen from one flower to the next, ensuring impollination and new plants. Some insects feed on pests, thus protecting plants. Others may carry disease or destroy entire harvests.

Caterpillars are larvae of butterflies and moths. Most species feed on plants. They have strong jaws to tear off and chew up plant matter. Sometimes caterpillars damage gardens or farmers' crops.

Caterpillar

The tiny **ladybird** can be a
useful insect. Many species
feed on insect pests, such as
aphids, scales and mites.
Farmers buy them in clusters
to help control these pests
on their farms.

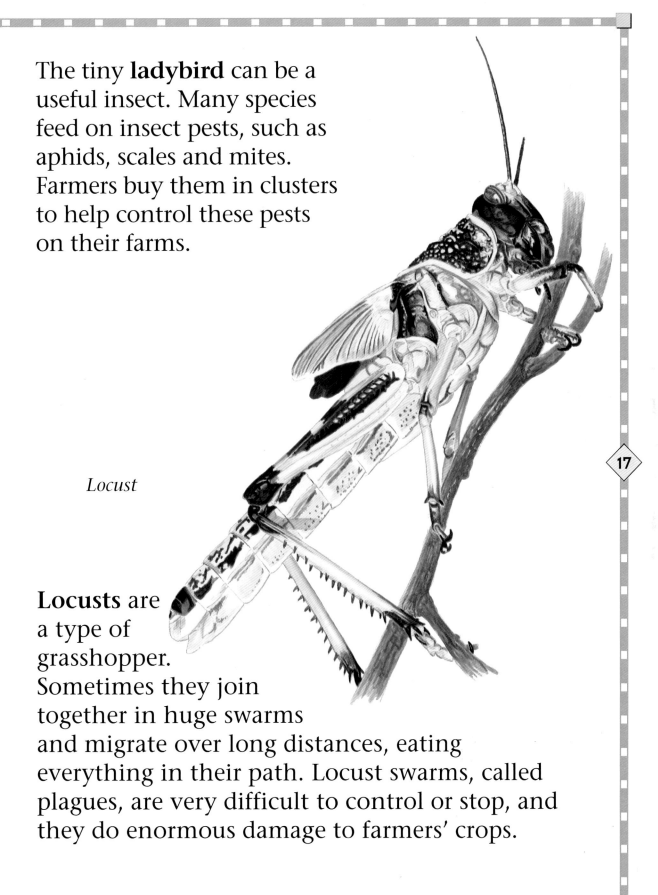

Locust

Locusts are
a type of
grasshopper.
Sometimes they join
together in huge swarms
and migrate over long distances, eating
everything in their path. Locust swarms, called
plagues, are very difficult to control or stop, and
they do enormous damage to farmers' crops.

PREDATORS

Many marine invertebrates are skillful hunters. Squid, cuttlefishes and octopuses are highly specialized predators. Fast-moving and more intelligent than other invertebrates, they feed on fish and crustaceans.

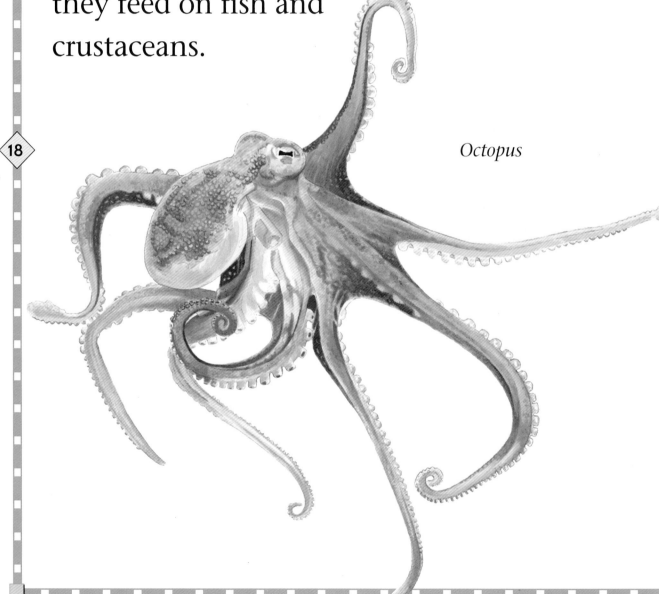

Octopus

Land leech

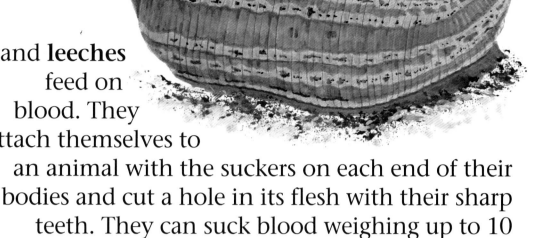

Land **leeches** feed on blood. They attach themselves to an animal with the suckers on each end of their bodies and cut a hole in its flesh with their sharp teeth. They can suck blood weighing up to 10 times their own body weight.

The **octopus** is a mollusc with eight tentacles or 'arms', each with two rows of powerful fleshy suckers. It lies in wait in holes or rocky crevices on the sea floor until some prey appears. It seizes its victim and injects it with a paralizing liquid. If an octopus is threatened, it sprays an inky substance into the water and escapes.

Invertebrate records

The giant squid is the largest living vertebrate. Over 18 metres across, each of its tentacles can measure up to 14 metres long. Among the insects, Goliath beetles from Central Africa are the heaviest, weighing up to 100 grams.

LIFE CYCLES

In some insects, such as grasshoppers, locusts or dragonflies, the adult is very similar to its young. In others, such as butterflies, flies, bees, wasps and beetles, each phase of life is marked by a transformation. This is called metamorphosis.

When a butterfly's eggs (1) hatch, a larva or caterpillar emerges (2). It changes its skin several times as it grows.

2

1

The caterpillar has little in common with the adult butterfly; they eat different foods and live in different habitats. Before turning into a chrysalis (3), the caterpillar seeks cover between two leaves or it weaves a silk cover.

The four main changes during complete metamorphosis.

The chrysalis (3) lives inside its protective shell for anywhere from a few days to two years, during which time it transforms itself by developing wings. At last, the adult butterfly (4) breaks out of the shell and flies away (usually for a very short life).

3

Swallow-tail butterfly

4

BLENDING IN

Many invertebrates, such as octopuses, jellyfish and spiders are skilled at blending into their surroundings. This enables them to hunt without being seen and to escape from predators.

The **crab spider** sits patiently on flowers waiting for insects in search of pollen. It can change its colour to match the host flower perfectly.

Crab spider

Leaf insects live in trees, bushes and on the stalks of plants. Their flat shapes, colour and the positions they adopt, make them almost invisible. They are closely related to stick insects, which are longer and thinner.

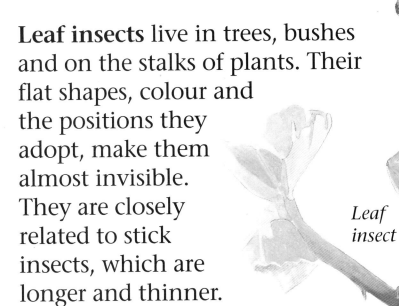

Leaf insect

Jellyfishes' transparent jelly-like bodies are hard to see in the water, making them lethal hunters. Their tentacles (up to 15 metres long) are armed with stinging cells which can kill small animals.

Jellyfish

GETTING ALONG

Invertebrates that share a habitat sometimes work together for their own and each other's advantage. In many cases they both benefit from the relationship.

Some **ants** and **aphids** help each other. The ants feed and protect large groups of aphids, in return for a sweet liquid which they 'milk' from the aphids.

Ant and aphid

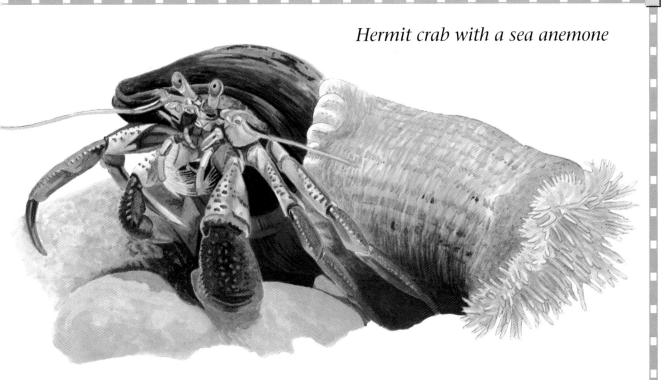

Hermit crabs have exposed abdomens. They often live in empty shells or other hollow objects for protection. To be even safer, they get a sea anemone to stick to the shell. Sea anemones are plant-like animals, with poisonous tentacles which protect the crab. The anemone is able to move about with the crab, so both species are benefited.

Ants

Most ants live in large colonies (some containing as many as 1 million individuals). Ant society is orderly, with the queen ants at the top of the hierarchy, followed by worker and male ants. Only queen ants and males can reproduce.

COMMUNICATION

Animals communicate using a number of different signals. They can warn each other of danger, pass on information about food sources, or communicate readiness to mate, among other things. Invertebrates are no exception; they also use sound, light, chemicals or even 'dance' to communicate.

When worker **bees** find a rich source of pollen they fly back to the hive to tell the others. They perform a kind of dance which gives information about the quantity of flowers and pollen, and the distance and the direction the swarm should take to find them.

The bee dance

Fireflies have light-producing organs on their abdomens. During mating, the male firefly does a kind of dance with special light signals and the female replies with her own luminous signals. The intensity of the light, the type of dance and the length of the signals differ from species to species.

Firefly

The male **fiddler crab** has one much larger and more brightly coloured claw than the other. By clicking his pincers he makes a noise which attracts the attention of female fiddler crabs and frightens rivals away.

Fiddler crab

INDEX